NUNCHAKU

NUNCHAKU
The Complete Training Guide
By Jiro Shiroma

UP

ISBN: 0-86568-091-4
Library of Congress Catalog Number: 87-50403

Designer: Danilo J. Silverio
Editor: Dave Cater

UNIQUE PUBLICATIONS
4201 Vanowen Place
Burbank, CA 91505

Acknowledgement

I would like to express my appreciation to the staff of Unique Publications for its help in making this book possible.

Table of Contents

O kinawa – Its History

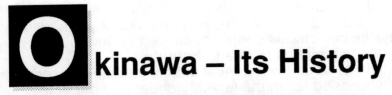

The origin and development of **kobu-do** (ancient fighting arts or karate weapons) is intimately tied to the Okinawan people who preserved its history and perfected its technique throughout the centuries.

The **Ryukyu** Islands (better known as Okinawa) is located approximately 175 miles southeast of Hong Kong and 450 miles southwest of Japan in the Pacific. Principally a farming area, the island is 75 miles long by 35 miles wide and has a population of 65,000.

Although early reports are sketchy, Okinawa's history can be traced back more than 1,800 years. Archaeologists have discovered remains dating back to A.D. 100. In Asian history books, the first mention of Okinawa comes in Chinese writings from A.D. 607. Japan followed by mentioning it in its records in A.D. 753.

For a period of 700 years beginning in A.D. 600, the island was the site of many battles as larger, seemingly more powerful nations sought to conquer its peace-loving people. In 1291, Kubla Khan's 6,000-man army, headed by General Yo Sho, stormed the shores of Okinawa. Surprisingly, it was soundly defeated. Five years later, Kubla Khan's army, this time led by General Cho Ko, met the same fate.

To survive the constant attack on its liberties, the Okinawan people began learning and mastering weapons techniques. Among the more popular weapons were the sword, spear, bo and staff.

In 1942, the king of the Ryukyu Islands, Sho Shin, ordered the Okinawan people to throw down their weapons. Faced with the need to defend themselves, but prohibited from carrying weapons, island warriors turned to an ancient form of empty-hand fighting arts called **Okinawa-te**.

At the same time, farmers, merchants and fishermen took up everyday tools to protect their lives and guard their property. The farmers chose the **kama**, **tonfa**, **nunchaku** and **bo**. Fisherman grabbed their **kai** (paddle) and merchants sided with the **hanbo** (a short bo, about four feet in length, which was used as a locking bar for sliding doors).

Almost 200 years later, Lord Simazu's Japanese army once again invaded Okinawa. This time they came with 3,000

1

samurai soldiers, 734 guns, 30,000 bullets and 117 bows. The island didn't stand a chance. But while the country was under foreign rule, its industrious people continued to develop and refine the techniques of **te** and **kobudo**.

The martial arts world owes a great debt of gratitude to a group of people who stood tall in the face of danger and perfected a fighting and weapons art that remains as strong today.

The Nunchaku

The first mention of the nunchaku can be found in ancient Chinese history, where two pieces of wood tied together by horse hair or piece of straw were used as horse bridles by mounted soldiers.

Their historical prominence, however, came into play more than 300 years ago on the **Ryukyu Islands** (better known as Okinawa). Until the 1600s, the nunchaku was not a martial arts weapon. In fact, it was a mere farm implement used by Okinawan commoners to beat rice or separate beans from their shells.

But necessity became the mother of invention when Japan, Okinawa's powerful neighbor to the northwest, flexed its muscles and invaded the tiny Pacific island. As they had during past invasions, the Japanese ruling party imposed a ban on all weapons, including those used in the practice of martial arts. This way, the Okinawans could not rebel.

Left only with their empty hands, the once peace-loving farmers began practicing Okinawa-te or kara-te (the martial art of the empty hand). They could practice in secrecy in the deep Okinawan jungles without fear of being caught and punished. At about the same time, farmers discovered that by using certain farm implements as extensions of their empty hands, their techniques were more powerful and their options limitless. Among the farm tools were the **nunchaku**, the **bo** (originally used to carry buckets of water) and the **sai** (a curved blade attached to a wood handle which cut grain stalks).

By using these innocent tools as deadly weapons, Okinawan people could carry these in the open without fear of discovery.

The approximate size and weight of the nunchaku has changed little in the past three centuries. Held together by a piece of rope or mental chain (early Okinawans used horse tail hair because a samurai's sword could not negotiate the thickness), each nunchaku stick measures between 13 and 14 inches in length and spands 1⅛ to 1¼ inches in diameter. The original nunchaku sticks were made from the core of a palm tree hardened three-to-five years in mud water. The wood became so hard after the constant soaking, it was unable to cut even with a samurai sword.

In the hands of a skilled practitioner, the nunchaku became an extension of the martial artist's hand. It weaved and ducked, snaked and slithered through an opponent's defenses. When properly used, it can transcend fixed dimensions.

Mastery of the nunchaku requires years of diligent training. Each single movement, each twist and spin, must be understood in its entirety before the practitioner can consider it his own. But once in the grasp of a highly trained tactician, it is a weapon with which to be reckoned. The nunchaku becomes a second pair of arms, slicing through an enemy's blocks and attacks with lightning quickness and deadly effectiveness.

Kata

Kata is considered both an internal and external exercise form. The external method regulates respiration, exercises the joints and muscles, teaches the art of self-defense (both from an offensive and defensive point of view), and unifies the harsh and gentle forces that exist throughout life. The internal method constitutes the training and conditioning of the body's joints and muscles.

Kata is considered the foundation of the art of Okinawan kobudo. Done without a partner, kata demands the ultimate in power, balance, coordination, breathing, confidence and humility.

The movements performed in a kata are singular in nature. But when combined, they form a fighting set which can be used in self-defense situations involving both empty hands and weapons sets. Performing forms for forms sake is not encouraged in Okinawan martial arts; it is the experience of generations of martial arts masters that true self-defense is possible only after serious and prolonged forms training.

echniques

SABURI

Self-practice of the weapon for the purpose of striking, swinging, thrusting or blocking in the air. The purposes of the subari are to build coordination, improve speed and skills, and strengthen your mental and physical conditioning. Practice "suburi" until it becomes a natural movement.

JODAN USHIRO SHIHEI KAMAE

From a ready stance (1), strike horizontally across the face (2-4) and continue to swing around the neck (5). Retrieve with the left hand (6). Also remember to practice with the left hand.

1

2

3

4

5

6

WAKI OTOSHI

From the ready position (1), strike diagonally upward across the body (2-4). Continue the circular motion clockwise and strike diagonally downward across the body (5). Retrieve with the left hand (6). Remember to practice with the left hand.

1

2

Continued

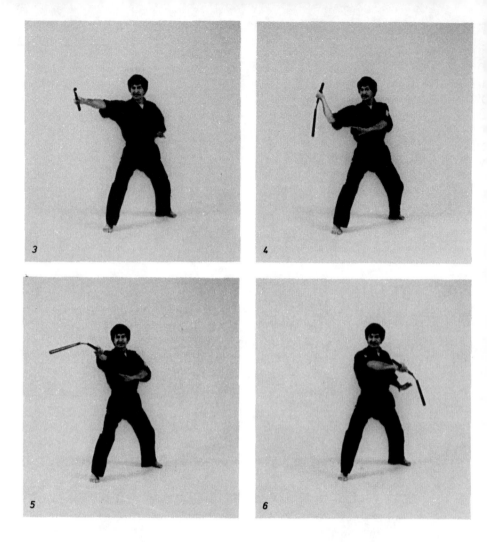

JODAN USHIRO SUIHEI KAMAE

From the on-guard position (1), strike diagonally across the body (2-4). Then stop the nunchaku with the left hand and strike diagonally across the body (5-6). Return the nunchaku over the right shoulder (7) and catch with the left hand (8). Continue swinging the nunchaku upward counterclockwise over the left shoulder (9-11). Return the nunchaku to the back of the body and catch it with the right hand (12). Also practice with the left hand.

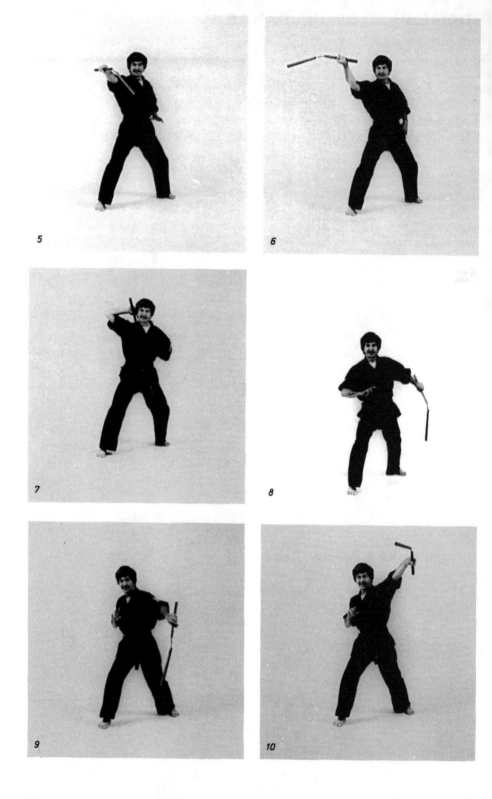

5

6

7

8

9

10

GYAKU KAMAE

From a ready stance (1), strike diagonally across the
body (2-3). Retrieve with the left hand (4). Also practice with
the left hand.

Continued

SINGLE FIGURE 8

From the left side (1), swing the nunchaku upward diagonally (2) across the body (3). Swing the nunchaku in a circular motion upward (4-5) and strike diagonally across the body (6-7). Return to the side of the body (8).

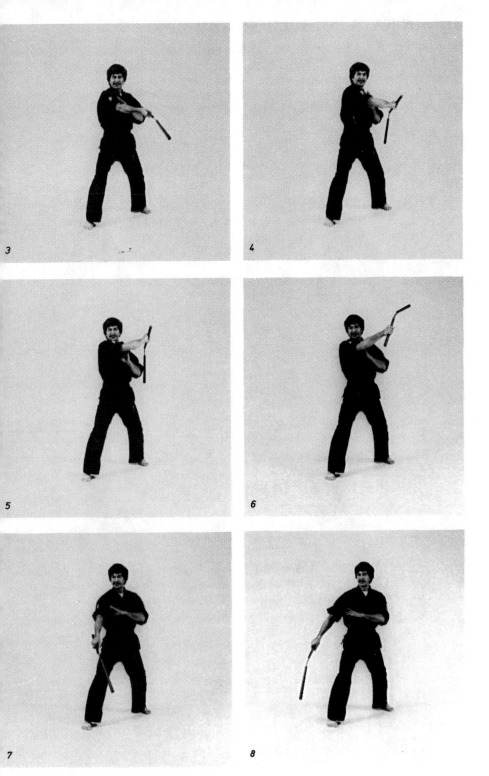

3

4

5

6

7

8

13

JODAN KATA (SHOULDER) KAMAE

Hold both sides of the nunchaku (1) and point the butt end toward the opponent's eye (2). Snap the wrist and throw straight (3). Snap back (4) and retrieve in the same hand.

CHUDAN KAMAE

Snap the wrist and strike forward (1-3). Snap back and circle upward (4-5) and retrieve with the same hand (6).

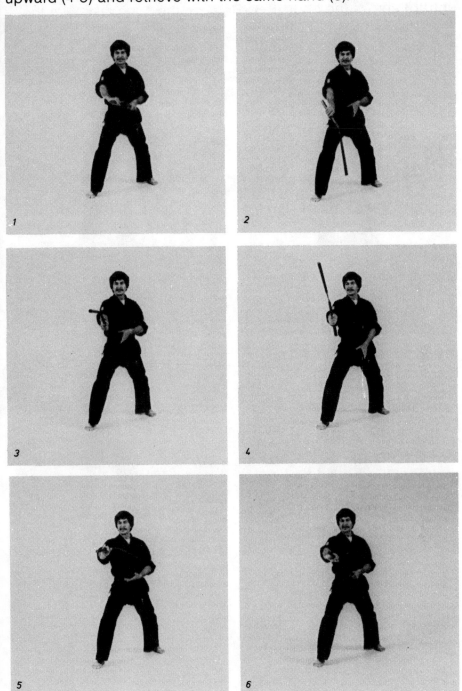

JODAN YOKO KAMAE

Strike diagonally upward across the body (1-4). Retrieve
the nunchaku with the right hand (5). Strike diagonally
upward across the body (6-8). Retrieve the nunchaku with the
left hand at the armpit (9).

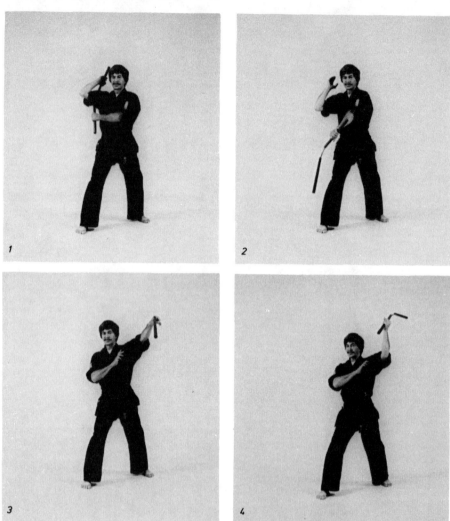

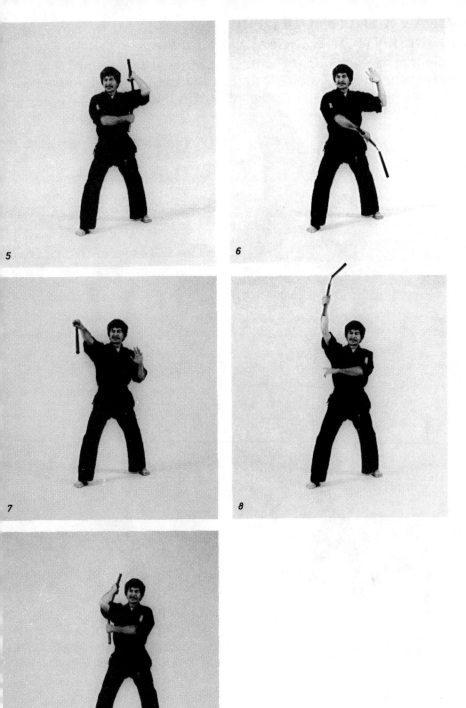

5

6

7

8

9

JODAN KATA (SHOULDER)
SASOI (ENTICING KAMAE)

From a ready position (1), strike horizontally across the body (2-4). Strike diagonally across the body (5-6). Retrieve the nunchaku with the opposite hand at the back of the shoulder (7).

AGAINST A KNIFE

Face your opponent in gedan suihei kamae (1). As he attacks your shoulder, step to the side and block his arm (2-3). Strike the side of his head with a reverse strike (4-7).

Face your opponent in gedan gyaku kamae stance (1) and as he attacks your face, block with a rising block (2-3). Strike his jaw with a left (4) and strike the side of his face with your right (5-7).

Face your opponent in a gedan gyaku kamae stance (1). As he attacks your face (2), strike his forearm with your nunchaku (3). Twist your body and strike his jaw with your left (4). Then strike the side with your right (5). Thrust toward his throat with the butt of your nunchaku (6-7).

3

4

7

AGAINST EMPTY HAND

Face your opponent in a gedan katate yoko kamae stance (1).
As your opponent attempts a punch, block his strike with
your free hand and strike the side of his face (2-4).

Face your opponent in a gedan suihei kamae stance (1).
As your opponent punches at your face, block to the side and
thrust to his throat (2-5).

Face your opponent in a gedan yoko sage kamae (1) and as he punches at your face, block with your free hand. Grab his wrist at the same time and thrust to his solar plexus (2-4).

The purpose of the pre-arranged kumite is to improve split-second decision in the training hall. Generally, defenders assume a horizontal stance to improve the speed of the footwork decision-making in a critical situation.

Face your opponent in a gedan suihei kamae stance (1).
As your opponent punches at your chest, step backward and
raise the arms (2-3). Block downward (4) and wrap the
cord around his wrist (5). Step forward and behind his leg (6).
Pull your opponent to the ground (7-9).

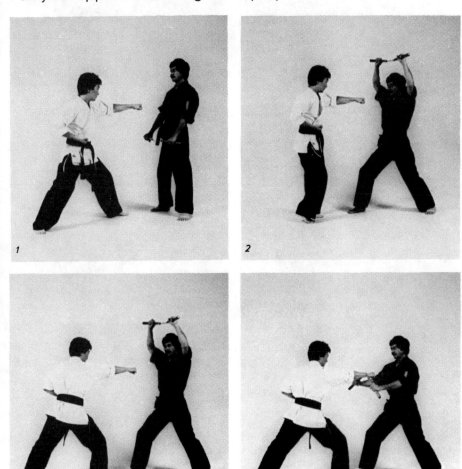

Continued

5

6

7

8

9

Face your opponent in a gedan suihei kamae stance (1).
As your opponent punches toward your face, step to the side
and block with your forearm (2-3). Push his wrist down
with the nunchaku, holding it with the same hand (4-5). Strike his
face with the nunchaku, holding the weapon in the opposite
hand (6-7).

Continued

Face your opponent in a gedan suihei kamae stance (1).
As your opponent punches at your face (2), block to the
side with your nunchaku cord (3). Thrust at his throat with the
butt ends of the nunchaku (4-5).

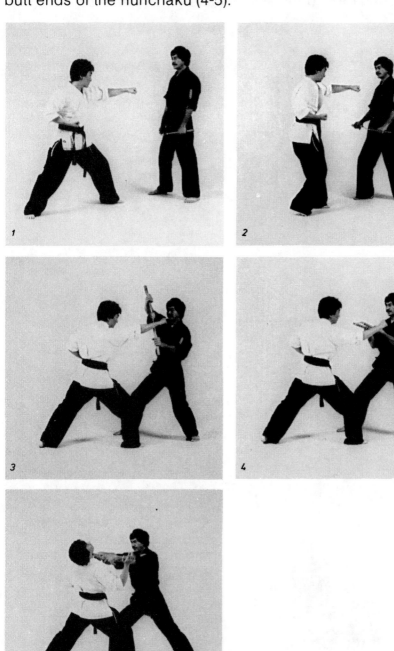

As your opponent grabs your right wrist (1), circle your
elbow upward (2) and grab the other end with your free hand (3).
Strangle his wrist with your arms and nunchaku (4). Pull him down
to the ground (5) and thrust with the ends of the nunchaku (6).

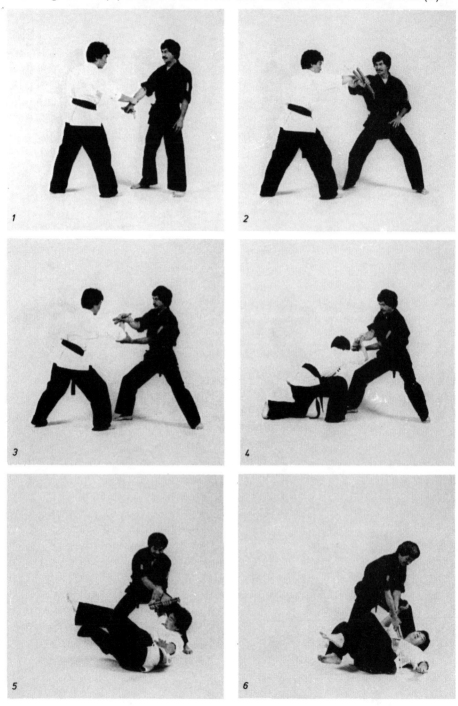

As your opponent grabs your outfit (1), raise your arms and nunchaku and place it between his arms (2). Pull the nunchaku down (3-4) and thrust the butt ends of the weapon into his throat (5-6).

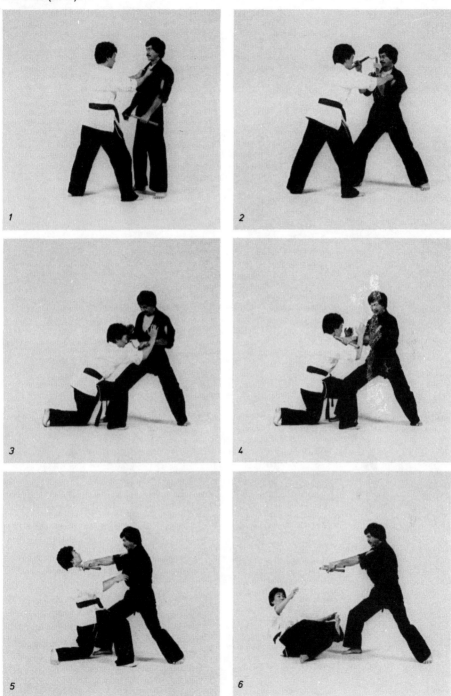

GYAKU (REVERSE HAND) WAKI OTOSHI

From a ready position (1), strike diagonally upward across the face (2-3). Swing the nunchaku in a circular fashion upward and strike diagonally downward across the face (4). Retrieve with the opposite hand in front of the body. Also practice with the opposite hand.

GYAKU WAKI OTOSHI

From the on-guard position (1), strike diagonally upward across the body (2-3). Strike horizontally across the face (4-5). Retrieve with the opposite hand (6). Raise the arm above the shoulders (7) and strike forward (8-9). Retrieve with the opposite hand (10-11).

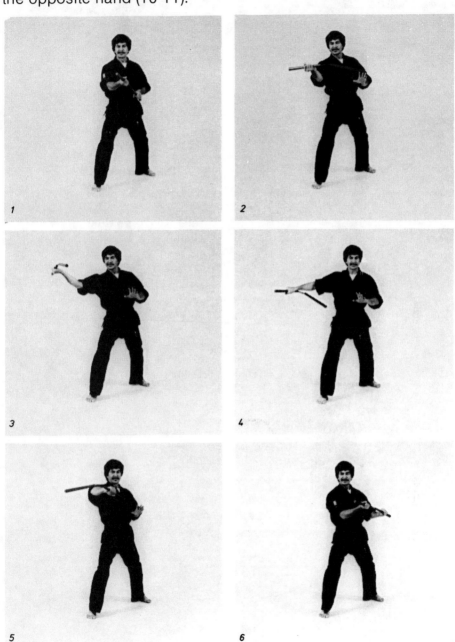

Continued

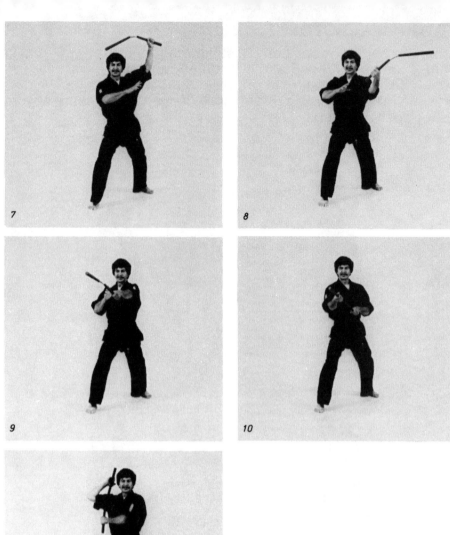

JODAN YOKO KAMAE FIGURE 8

From the ready position (1), strike diagonally downward across the body (2-3). Continue swinging the nunchaku in a circular upward fashion to above the shoulder (4). Strike diagonally downward at the side of the body (5). Continue swinging the nunchaku in a circular motion upward above the shoulder (6-7) and retrieve with the opposite hand.

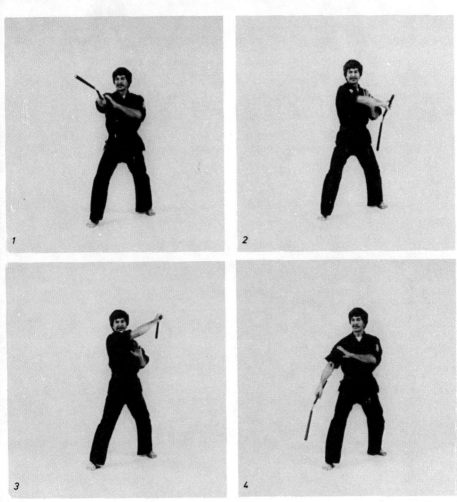

Continued

JODAN YOKO KAMAE

From the start position (1), strike forward downward at the side of the body (2-4). Twist the wrist to the right and continue swinging the nunchaku in an upward circular motion until you arrive at the shoulder (5-6). Strike forward (7-8). Twist the wrist to the left, swinging the nunchaku upward (9). Retrieve with the same hand (10).

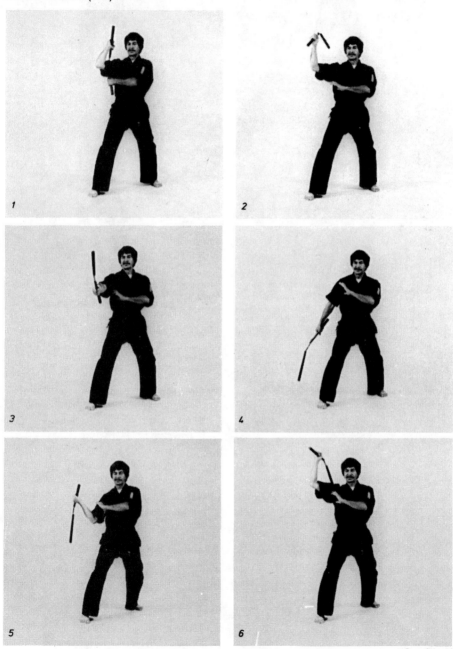

Continued

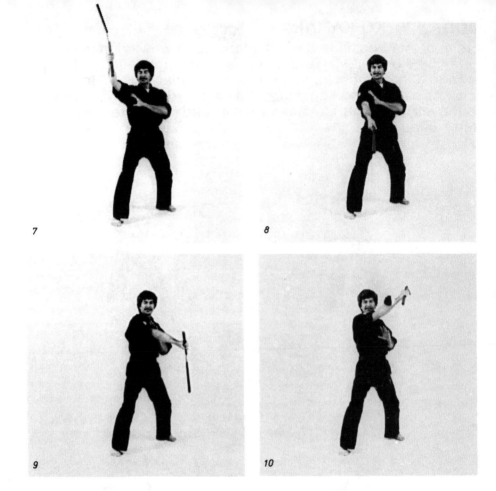

7

8

9

10

The purposes of kamae are to learn the movements and then practice handling the weapon in different stances.

KAMAE -- Stance.

JODAN NO KAMAE -- Stance placing the weapon higher than the shoulder.

CHUDAN NO KAMAE -- Stance placing the weapon in the middle section (between hip high to shoulder high).

GEDAN NO KAMAE -- Stance placing the weapon below the hip line.

SEIGAN NO KAMAE -- Point the edge of the weapon toward the opponent's eye.

KATATE KAMAE -- Holding the weapon with one hand.

MOROTE KAMAE -- Hold the weapon with both hands.

JUJI KAMAE -- X-stance.

KASUMI NO KAMAE -- Stance where the practitioner hides his eyes behind his arms or the weapon so the opponent can't read his mind.

KOWAKI KAMAE -- Stance placing the weapon under the armpit.

WAKI OTOSHI -- Stance placing the weapon on the side of the body below the hip line.

SASOI KAMAE -- Enticing stance (entice the opponent into a trap).

SUIHEI KAMAE -- Stance holding the weapon horizontally.

KAKUSHI KAMAE -- Stance hiding the weapon from the opponent's eye.

YOKO KAMAE -- Stance placing the weapon on the side of the body.

MUSO KAMAE -- (Stance of mind of no mind). Any stance can be muso kamae.

MUKAMAE NO KAMAE -- (Stance of no stance). Generally, the hand holds the nunchaku lower and at the side of the body.

Note: All stances can be performed with the left or right foot forward, or in the horizonal stance.

CHUDAN MOROTE KAMAE
(Hidari Hanmi--Chest Point)

Front View   Side View

JODAN MOROTE KAMAE
(Hidari Hanmi)

Front view   Side View

JODAN YOKO KAMAE
(Hidari Hanmi)

Front view   Side view

CHUDAN MOROTE KAMAE
Migi Hanmi -- Chest Point
(Right 45-degree angle)

Front   Side view

JODAN MOROTE KAMAE
(Migi Hanmi)

Front view   Side view

JODAN YOKO KAMAE

Front view   Gyaku (Reverse) jodan
                              yoko kamae

MIGI (RIGHT) KOWAKI KAMAE

Front view   Side view

CHUDAN MOROTE KAMAE
(Wrap the cord or chain around the arm. This is one way
to hold the weapon).

Front view   Side view

KASUMI KAMAE
(Hide the eyes from the opponent).

Front view

Side view

CHUDAN SASOI KOSHI KAMAE

Back view

Side view

JŌDAN SASOI SUIHEI KAMAE

Front view

Back view

KAKI OTOSHI KAMAE

Front view

Side view

SEIGAN NO KAMAE

Front view   Side view

SHIHO (SQUARE) KAMAE

Front view   Side view

MUSUBI KAMAE

Front view

Side view

CHUDAN KATATE KAMAE

Front view

Side view

NICHO NUNCHAKU
JODAN KAMAE

From the ready position (1), raise the right foot (2) and swing the nunchaku in a circular motion downward at the side of the body (3). Step forward (4) and strike diagonally downward with the opposite nunchaku (5-6). Circle the wrist in front of the body and raise the arm above the shoulder. (7). Raise the left foot (8) and swing the nunchaku in a downward circular motion at the side of the body (9-10). Step forward (11) and strike diagonally downward across the body (12-13). Then prepare for the next offensive and defensive movements (14).

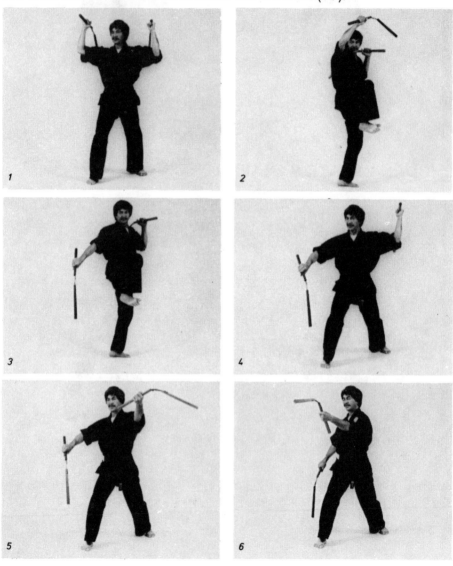

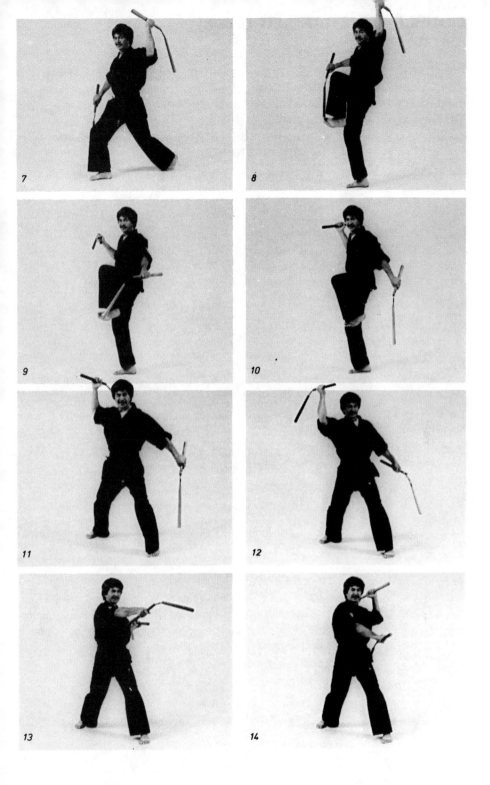

DOUBLE NUNCHAKU FIGURE 8
JODAN KAMAE

From a ready stance (1), raise the arms (2) and strike diagonally across the body with both nunchaku simultaneously (3-4). Continue swinging in an upward circular motion at the side of the head (5). Strike diagonally downward (6). Continue the swing, opening the arms to the side (7). Swing the nunchaku in a circular motion (8-9) and retrieve the weapon with the armpits (10-11). Complete the figure eight.

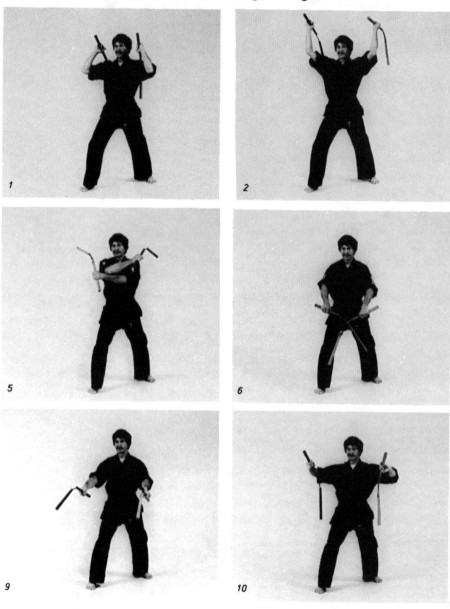

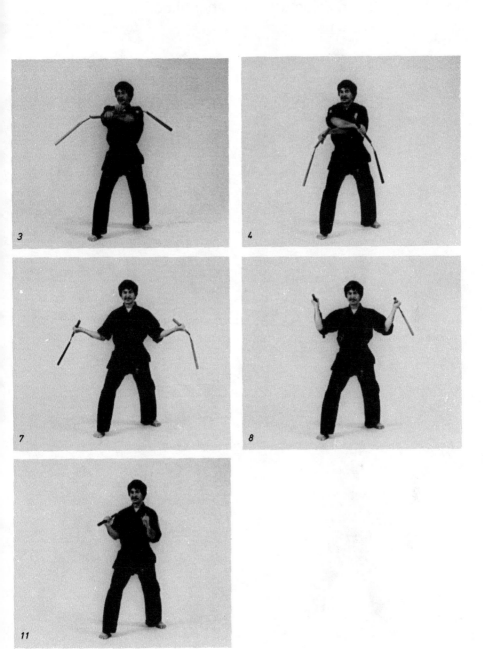

JODAN YOKO KAMAE

From the on-guard position (1), strike diagonally downward across the body with the nunchaku, holding it with the right hand (2-3). At the same time, strike diagonally upward across the body with the nunchaku in the left hand (4-6). Then strike diagonally downward across the body with the nunchaku in the right hand. Do the same with the other hand.

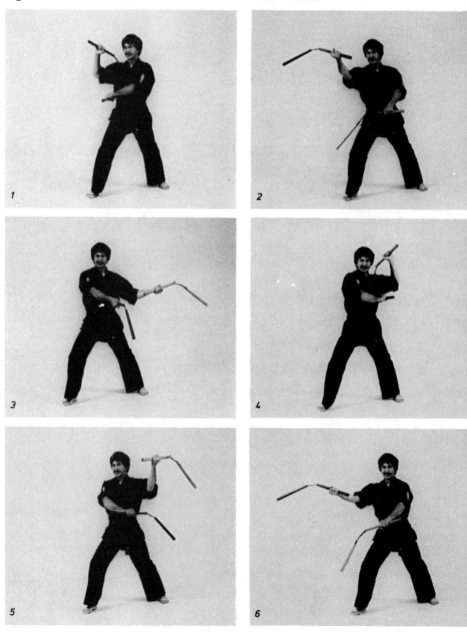

56

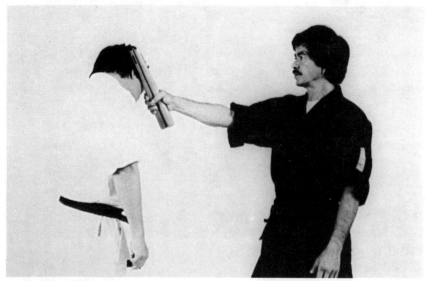

Strike the temple.

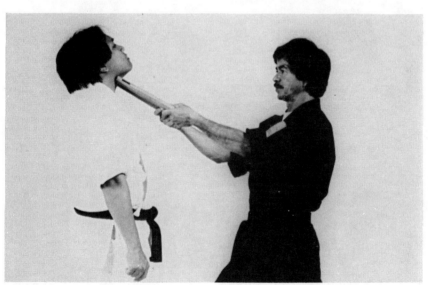

Thrust at the throat with the
ends of the nunchaku.

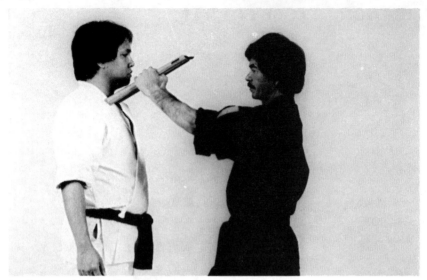

Strike at the collarbones with
the butt ends of the nunchaku.

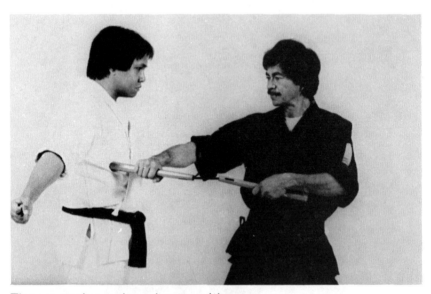

Thrust at the solar plexus with
the butt end of the nunchaku.

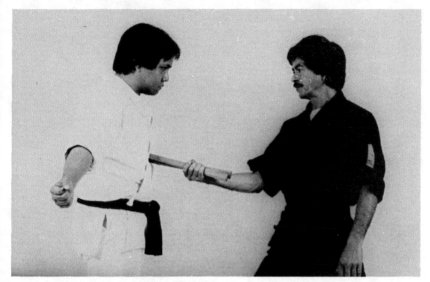

Thrust at the solar plexus with
the ends of the nunchaku.

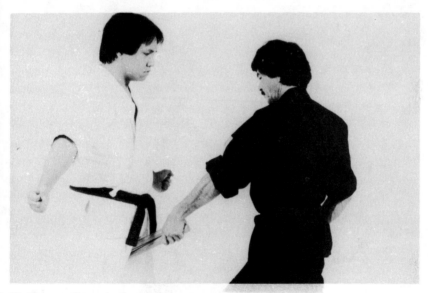

Strike at the groin area.

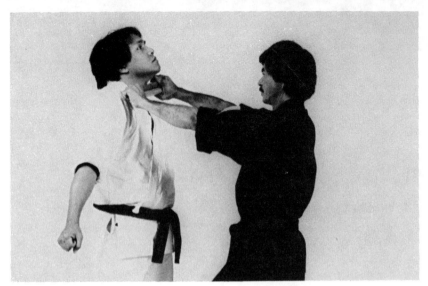

Strike at the throat.

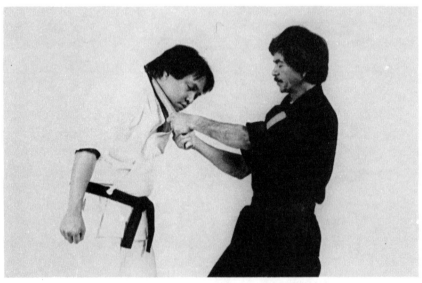

Wrap the back and front of the
neck with the nunchaku
(sleeperhold).

Wrap the neck from behind with
the nunchaku (sleeperhold).

Pull and choke from behind.

Pull and press the nose
and eyes.

Pull with the right and push
the opponent off balance.

Elbowlock.

Wristlock (with cord or chain).

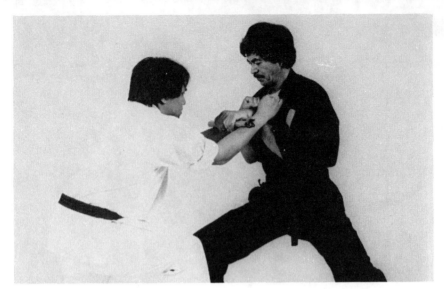

Double wristlock.

Armlock.

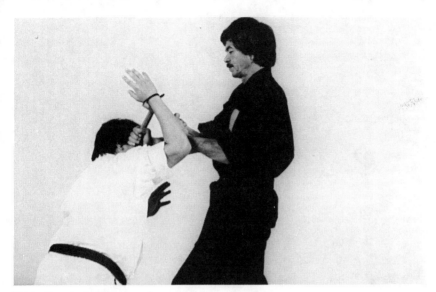

Wristlock (with cord or chain).

Wristlock.

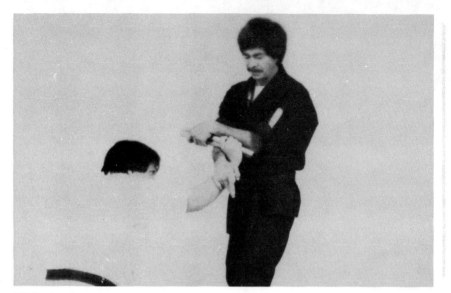

Wristlock.

Wristlock (with cord or chain).

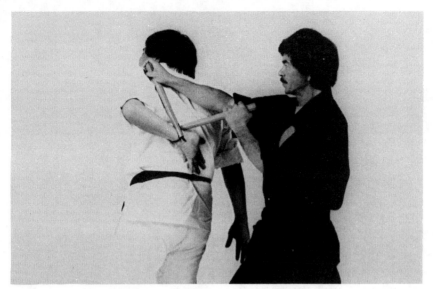

Wrist and armlock from behind.

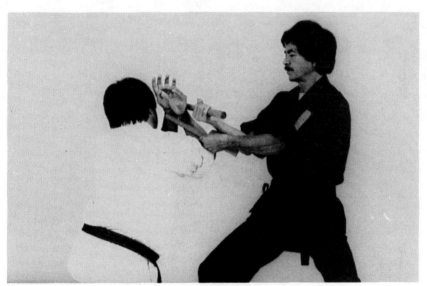

Double wristlock.

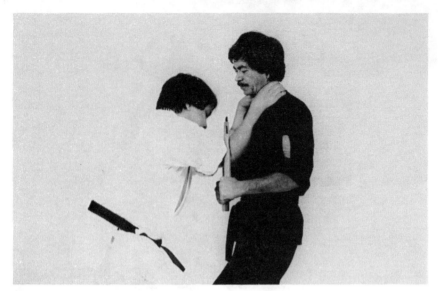

Double elbowlock against
front chokehold.

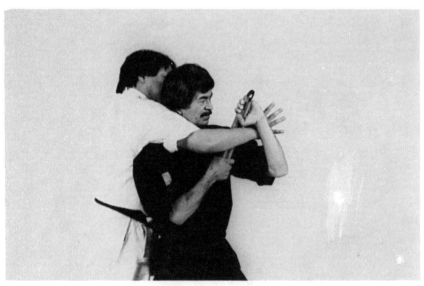

Wristlock against chokehold.

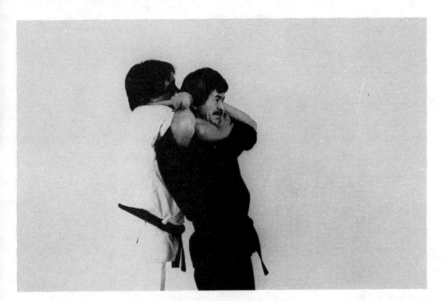

Nunchaku sleeperhold against
arm chokehold.

Shoulderlock.

Elbowlock and shoulderlock.

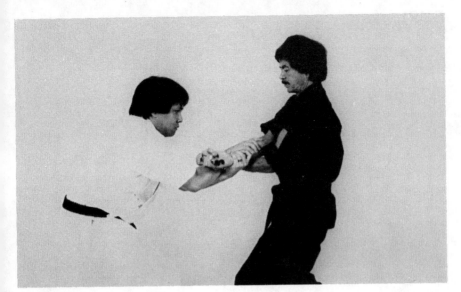

Armlock.

SUBURI
CHUDAN MOROTE KAMAE
From a ready stance (1), strike diagonally across the body (2-4) and retrieve with the left hand (5).

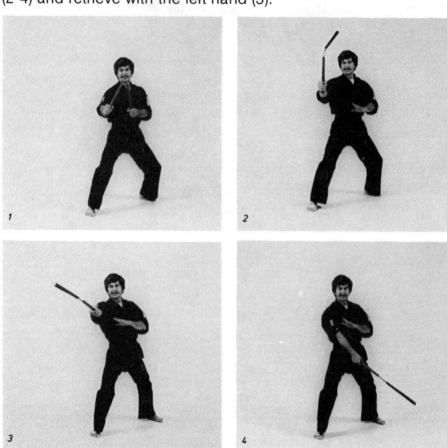

JODAN KAMAE

From the ready position (1), initiate a circular strike to the side of the head (2-4). Retrieve with the left hand (5). Remember to practice with the opposite hand.

YOKO KAMAE

From the start (1), strike downward at the side of the body (2-4)
Swing the nunchaku back over the right shoulder (5) and
retrieve with the left hand (6). From the same position (7), strike
horizontally across the body (8-9) and swing the nunchaku
upward with the right hand (10). Also start the exercise with the
left hand(11).

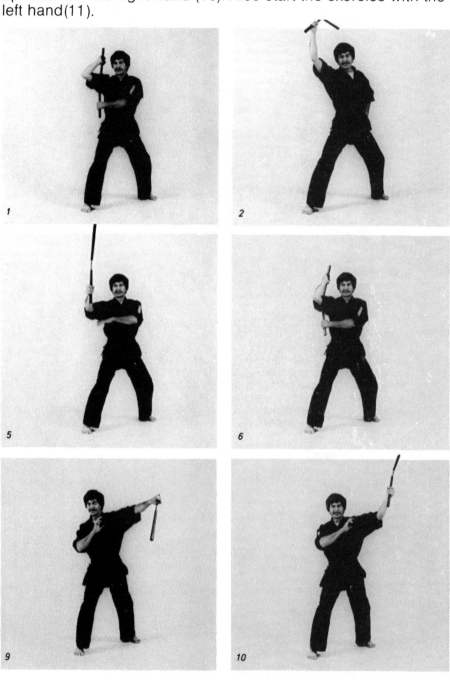

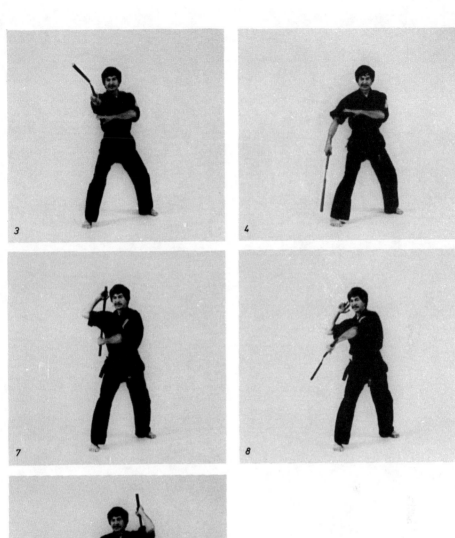

CHUDAN SASOI KOSHI KAMAE

From the beginning (1), strike upward at the side of the head (2-3). Following a swinging circle (4), strike diagonally across the body (5) and catch the nunchaku with the left hand (6). Also practice this move with the left hand.

KOWAKI KAMAE

In this kowaki kamae exercise (1), strike forward (2-3) and bring the nunchuku under the armpit (4-5). Also practice with the other hand.

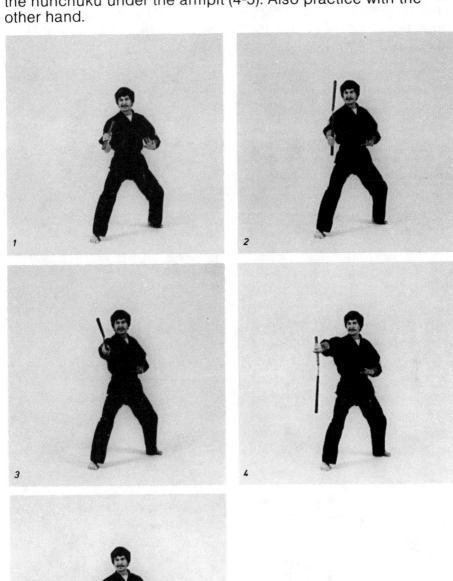

AGAINST THE BO

Face your opponent in a chudan seigan kamae stance (1). As your opponent thrusts at your throat, step to the side and block to the opposite side (2). Strike his body with both sides of the nunchaku (3-6). Raise the arms (7-8) and strike to the back of the neck (9-10).

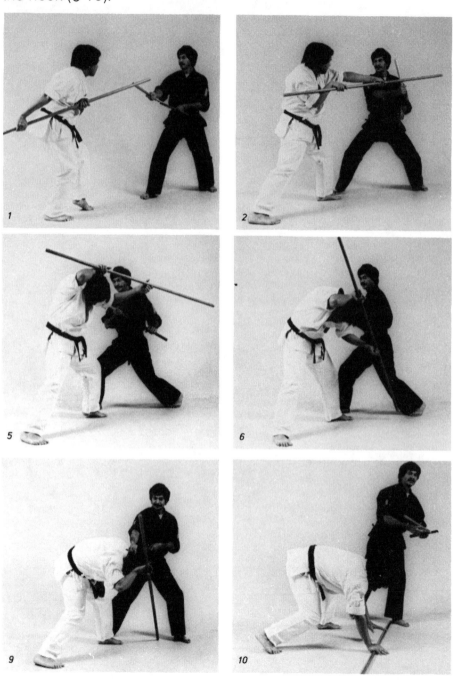

AGAINST THE NUNCHAKU

Face your opponent in a jodan yoko kamae stance (1). As your opponent aims for the side of your head (2), strike his cord (or chain) with your cord (or chain) (3). With your cord (or chain), entangle his cord (4). Pull the nunchaku down to unbalance and disarm your opponent (5). Strike diagonally upward to the side of his face with two nunchaku (6-7). Then strike downward to the back of his neck (8).

Face your opponent in a gedan muso (mind of no mind or stance of no stance) stance. (1). As your opponent goes for the side of your body, step backward and block (2-3). Wrap your nunchaku around his weapon (4) and disarm him (5). Thrust at his throat (6-7) and strike his eyes with the butts of your weapon (8).

Face your opponent in a waki otoshi stance (1). As he strikes at your leg (2), step backward and strike downward with your nunchaku (3). Raise the arm (4) and strike his head (5-6).

Face your opponent in a gedan suihei kamae stance (1). As your opponent moves to strike your head (2), drop down to one knee and strike upward into his groin (3). Continue swinging the nunchaku at the side of your shoulder (4) and strike the side of his neck (5).

KATA

Start in a chudan morote kamae stance (1) and strike forward (2-3). Continue swinging the nunchaku in a downward circular motion (4). Retrieve with the left hand (5). Raise the arms above the head (6) and strike horizontally in a circular counterclockwise motion (7-8). Retrieve with the left hand (9). Push forward horizontally (suihei in kamae) (10) and switch the stance to jodan yoko kamae (11-12). Strike forward and downward (13-14) at the side of the body (15). Swing the nunchaku in a circular upward motion (16-17). Retrieve with the left hand (18). Switch the stance in jodan yoko kamae (19-20). Strike horizontally across the left side of the body (21). Continue swinging the weapon in a circular upward motion (22-23). Retrieve the nunchaku with the right hand (24) and you'll be in a hidari (left) gyaku (reverse) jodan yoko kamae. Swing the nunchaku in a figure-eight motion (25-29). Continue swinging the nunchaku and bring it behind the neck. Retrieve with the left hand (30). Strike diagonally downward across the body (31-33). Then strike diagonally upward across the body above the opposite shoulder. Wrap it around your neck. Retrieve with the right hand (34-35). Strike in a circular motion at the opponent's leg (36-37). Swing upward in a circular clockwise movement (38-39). Assume the jodan migi (right) yoko kamae stance (40). Strike forward and downward between the thighs (41-42). Retrieve with the left hand (43) and continue swinging in a circular upward motion (44-45) above the shoulder (46). Retrieve with the right hand (47) in the gyaku jodan yoko kamae stance. Bring the nunchaku in front of the chest (48-49). Thrust with both ends of the nunchaku (50) and strike horizontally across the body (51-52). Immediately thrust with the butt end of the nunchaku (53-54). Pull the nunchaku back to the side by the waist and assume the waki otoshi kamae stance (55). Step forward with left foot stance in yama (mountain) kamae (56). Step forward into chudan morote kamae stance (57). Strike forward (58-61). Retrieve with your left hand (62). Bring the nunchaku to the side of your shoulder (63-64). Strike forward (65-66).

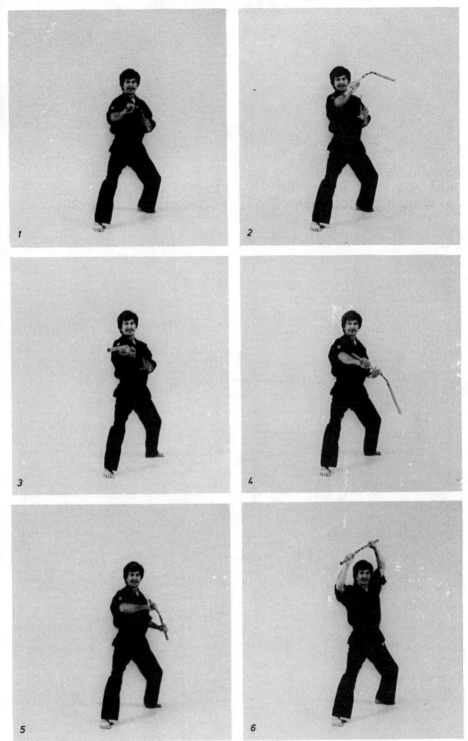

Continued

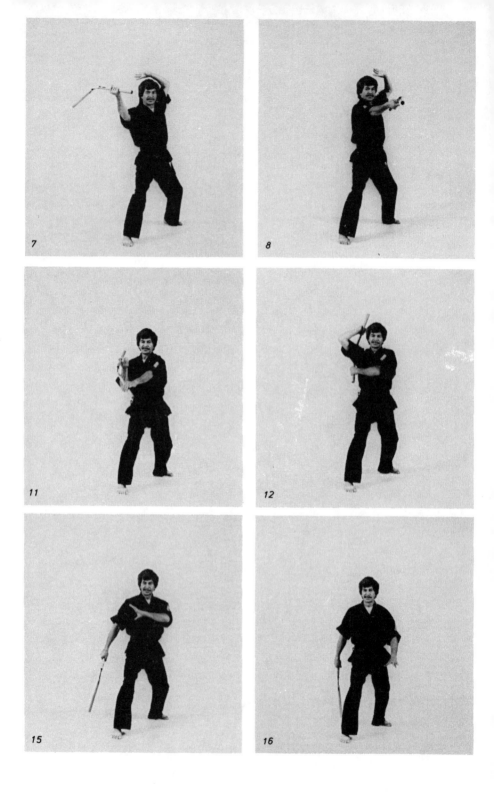

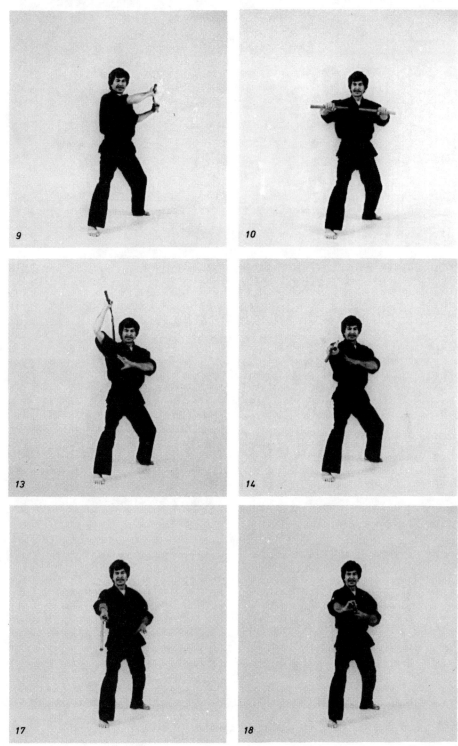

Continued

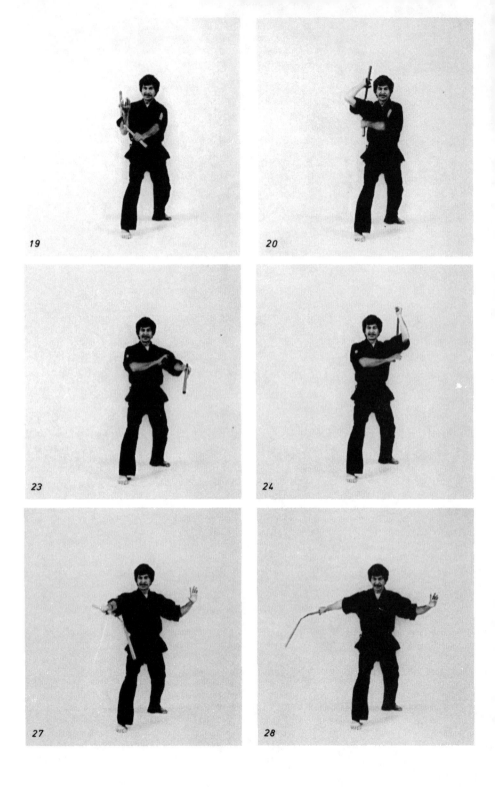

19 01990 2020 2023 2424 2727 2828

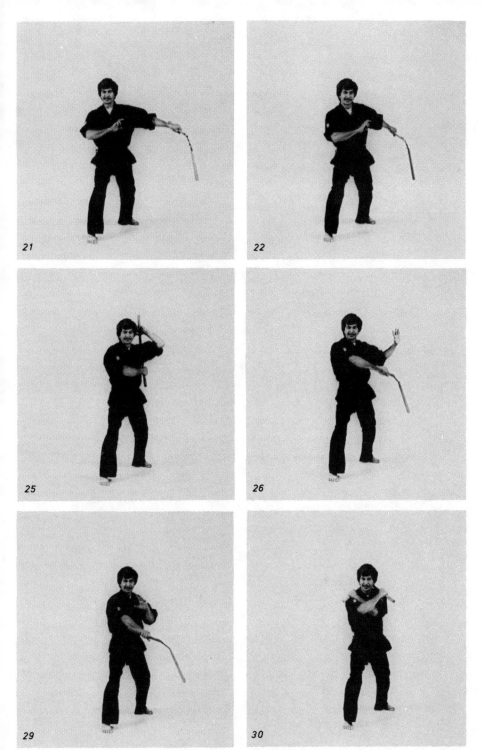

21

22

25

26

29

30

Continued

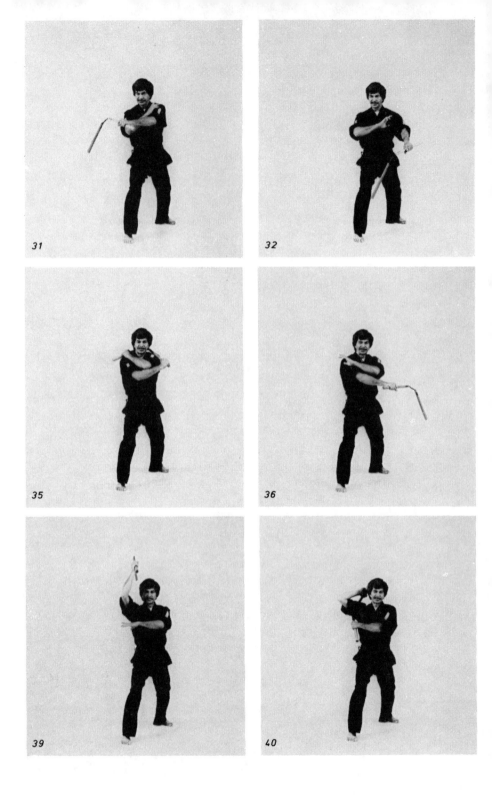

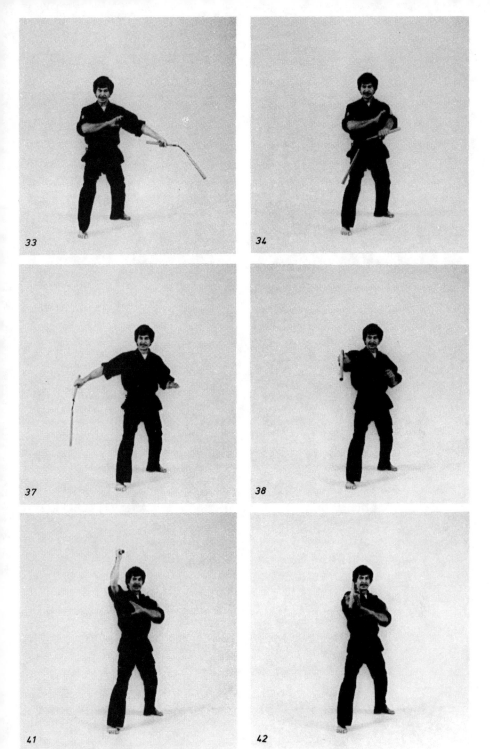

Continued

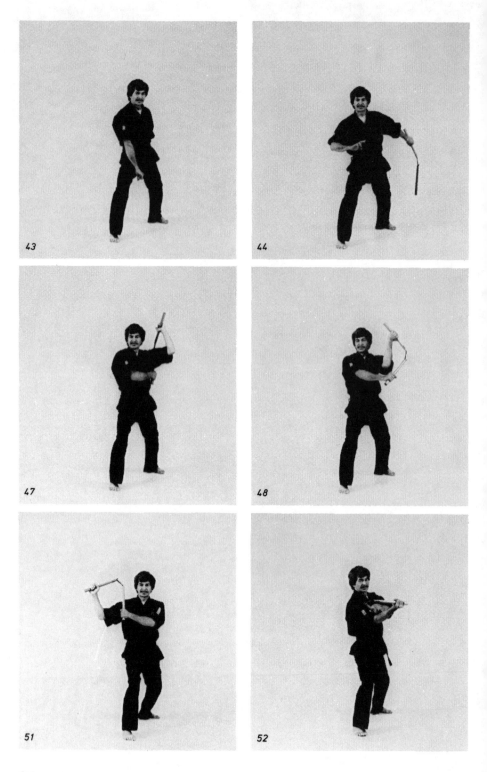

43

44

47

48

51

52

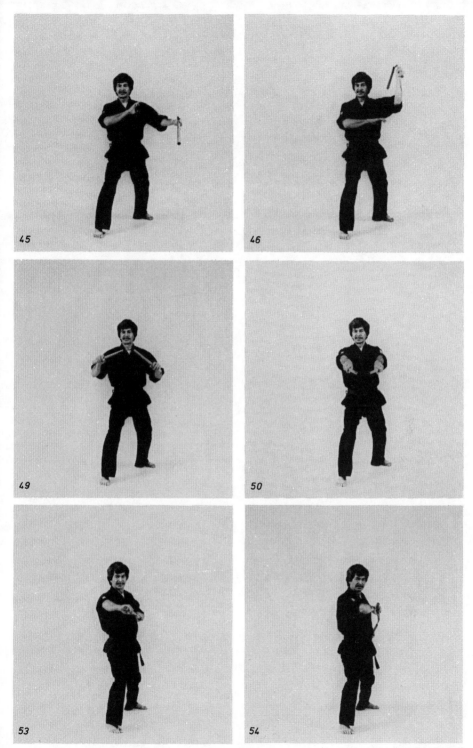

Continued

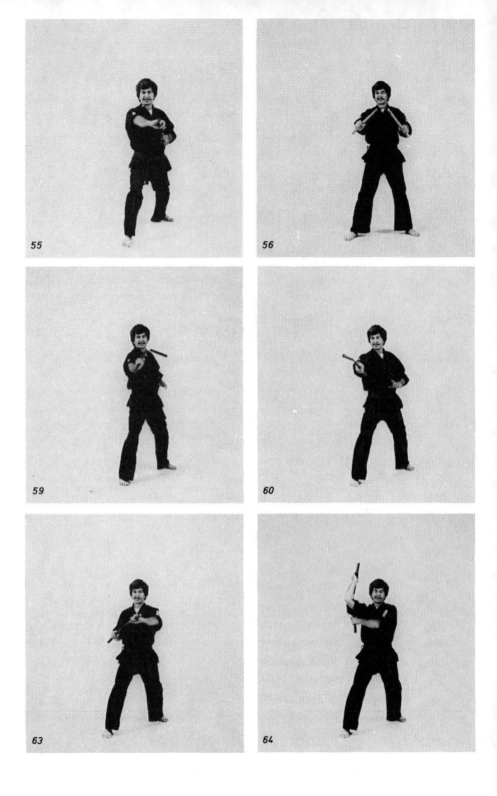

55

56

59

60

63

64

96

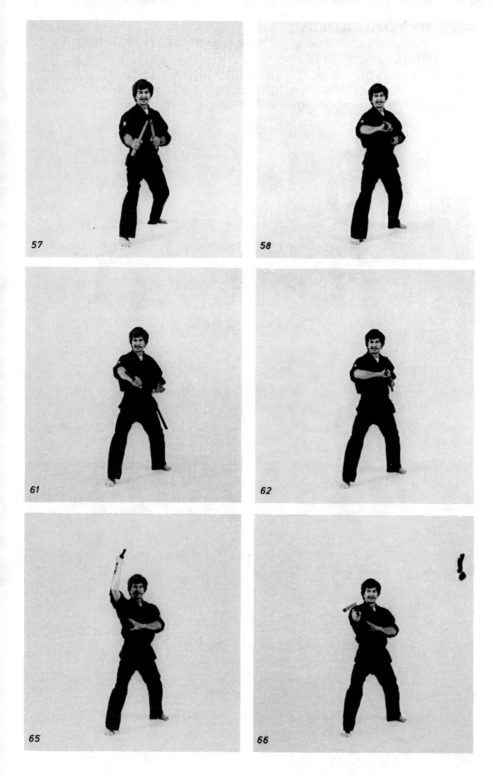

JODAN YOKO KAMAE

From the ready position (1), strike forward (2-3) and bring the nunchaku to the side of the leg (4). Swing the nunchaku upward over your shoulder (5-6) and retrieve the weapon with your left hand (7). Then switch your stance to the suihei kamae stance. Also practice with the left hand.

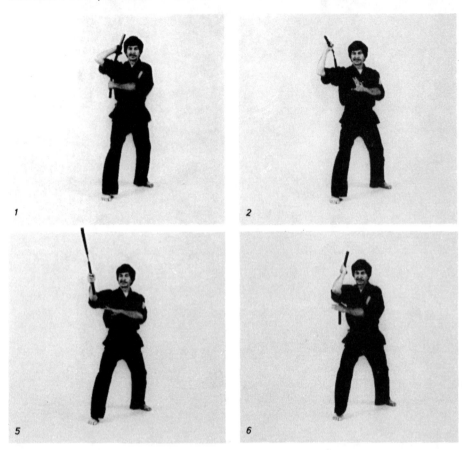

CHUDAN NO KAMAE

From the ready position (1), switch stances to the jodan yoko kamae stance (2-3). Strike downward and forward to the center (4-5). Bring it to the right and under the body between the thighs (6). Catch the nunchaku behind the body with the left hand (7). Swing the nunchaku upward over the shoulder (8-10) and retrieve the nunchaku with the right hand (11). This stance is called gyaku (reverse) jodan yoko kamae. Now return to the beginning stance (12-13). Also practice with the opposite hand.

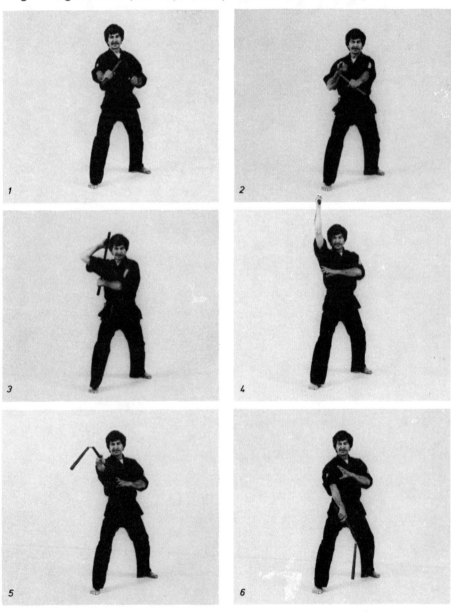

WAKI OTOSHI KAMAE

From the beginning stance (1), strike in a circular motion diagonally across the body (2-4). Continue swinging the nunchaku (5) in a circular upward motion above the shoulder and retrieve with the left hand--hidari (left) yoko kamae (6). Strike diagonally downward across the body (7-10). Continue swinging the nunchaku in an upward circular motion (11). Then retrieve the weapon with your right hand (12). Strike diagonally downward across the body (13-16) and catch the nunchaku with the left hand (17). Stop in the chudan kamae stance (18). Start with the opposite hand to build coordination in both the left and right hands.

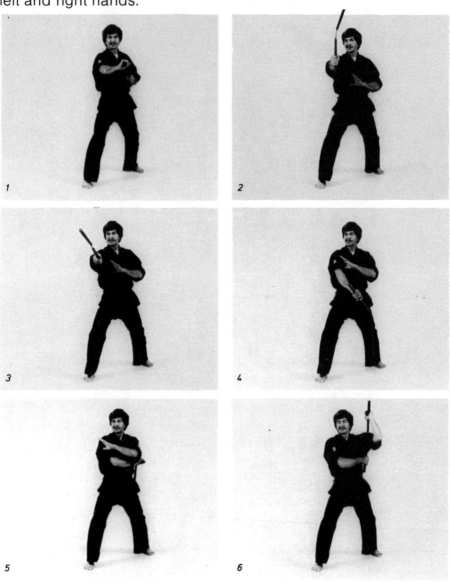

1

2

3

4

5

6

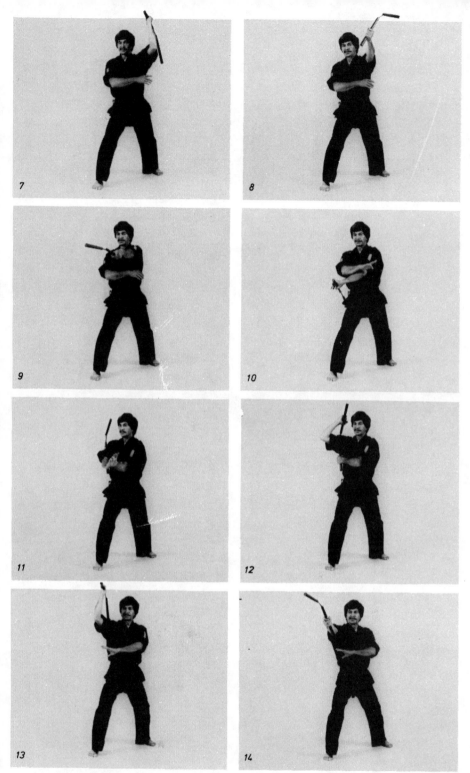

Continued

AGAINST EMPTY HAND

Face your opponent in gedan suihei kamae stance (1). As your opponent attempts to strike your face (2), block with a raising block (3) and wrap the nunchaku around his wrist. Strangle tightly and pull down to the side (4-6).

As your opponent grabs your wrist (1), circle your arm upward in a counterclockwise motion (2-3). Lock his left wrist and pull down toward the ground (4-5). Thrust toward him with the ends of the nunchaku (6).

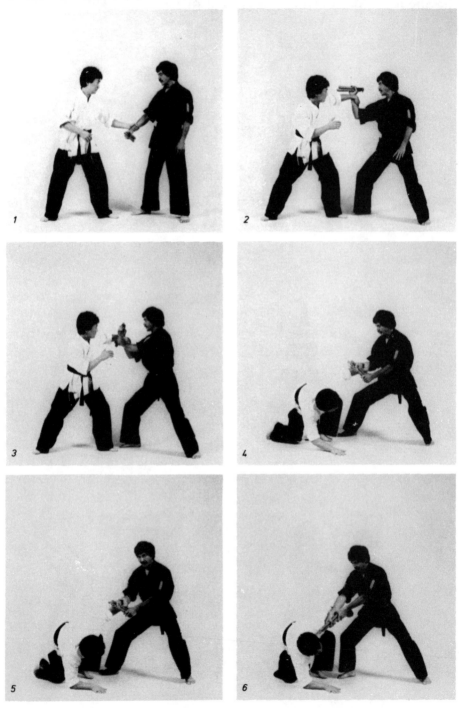

As your opponent grabs your wrists, assume the gedan suihei-kamae stance (1). Push your arm diagonally upward to break his hold (2-3). Immediately circle your opposite arm counter-clockwise and upward and twist his arm (4). As he bends forward, knee him in the face (5).

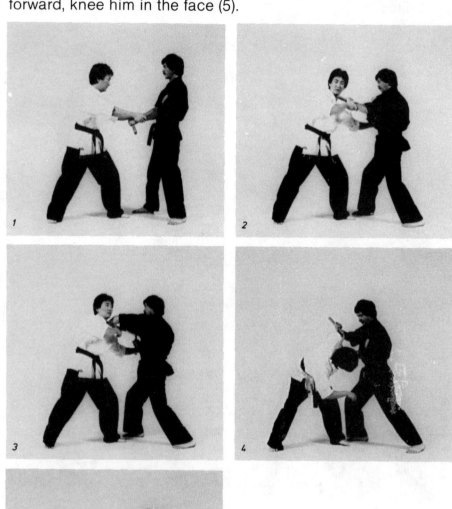

Face your opponent in a gedan suihei kamae stance (1). As your opponent punches at your face (2), block downward with the cord (3). Wrap his wrist around and strangle tightly. Spin your body under the opponent's arm (4-5) and throw him to the ground (6-7).

As your opponent grabs your wrist (1), circle your arm upward and outside of his arm (2). Lock his wrist with your nunchaku (3) and pull him to the ground (4).

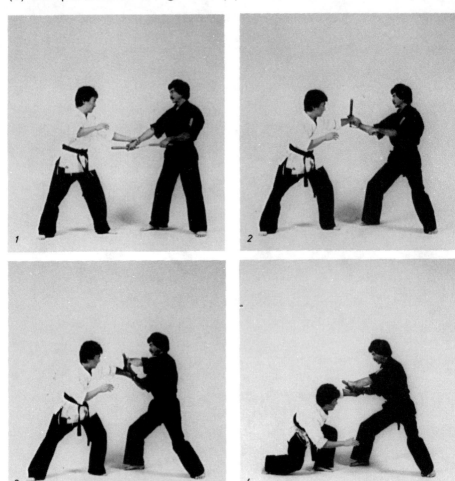

Face your opponent in a gedan suihei kamae stance (1). As he kicks at you, block downward (2-3). Wrap his ankle with your nunchaku (4). Twist your body and throw him to the ground.

JIYU SUBURI (To freely strike in the air)

Jiyu suburi means to practice in a free, uninhibited motion. Free -- strike after strike, swing after swing, stance to stance. The practitioner should be in a free motion from three-to-five minutes.

JODAN YOKO KAMAE

From a ready stance (1), strike forward (2-3) and downward to the center (4). Continue swinging the nunchaku under the body between the thighs (5). Retrieve it with the left hand (6). Swing the nunchaku in a circular upward motion (7-8) over the shoulder (9) and catch the nunchaku with the left hand. Also practice with the left hand.

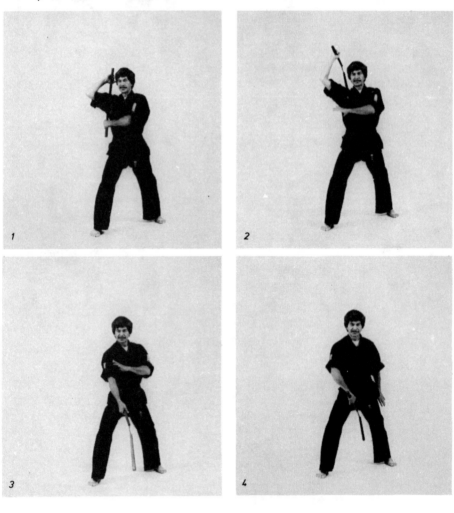

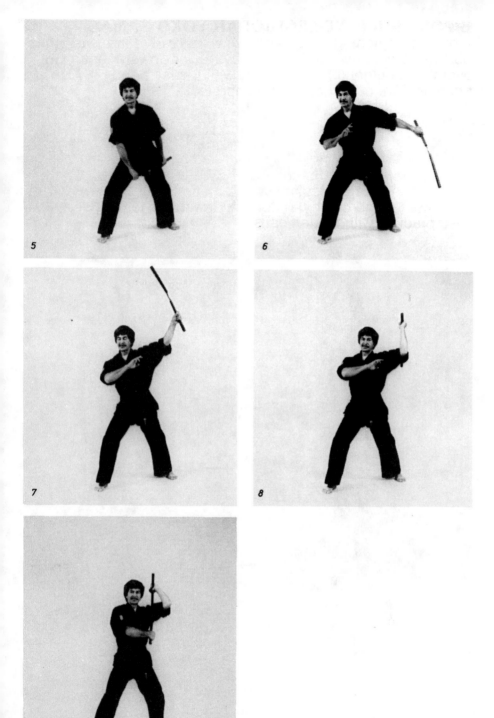

IPPON ASHI (ONE-LEG) JODAN YOKO KAMAE

From the beginning (1), strike downward (2-3) at the side of the body (4). Swing the nunchaku in a circular upward motion (5) over the shoulder (6) and retrieve with the left hand (7). Also practice with the opposite hand and leg.

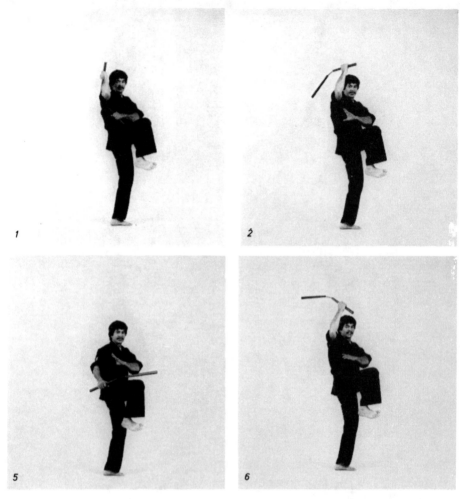

1

2

5

6

NICHO NUNCHAKU (DOUBLE NUNCHAKU)

Start in a kowaki kamae (1). Strike forward and downward (2-4).
Bring the nunchaku to the armpit (5). Strike forward and
downward with the opposite hand (6-8). Bring the nunchaku to
the armpit (9). Strike forward and downward simultaneously with
both nunchaku (10-11). Bring both nunchaku to the armpit
simultaneously (12-13).

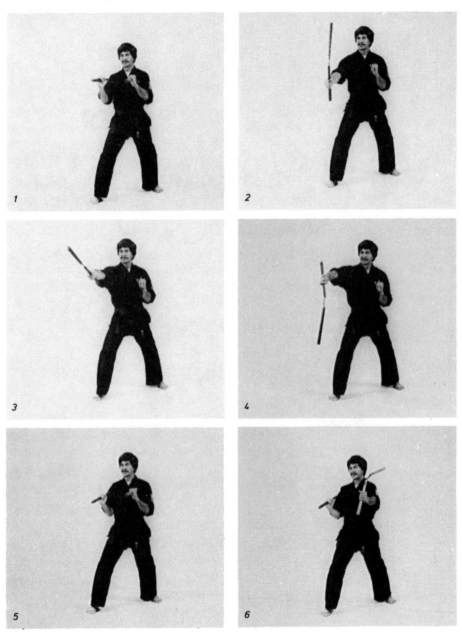

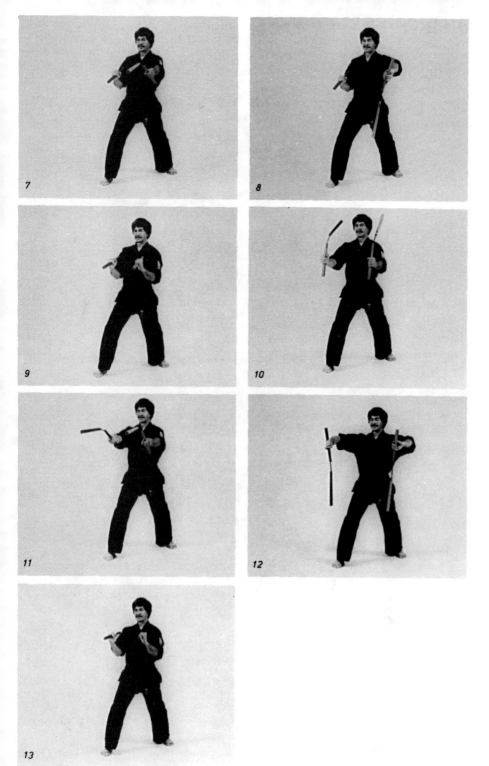

AGAINST EMPTY HAND

As your opponent kicks at your midsection, block downward with the cord (1). Wrap the nunchaku around his ankle and strangle tightly, pulling him to the ground (2).

Face your opponent in a gedan suihei stance (1). As he kicks at your midsection, thrust at his shin with the ends of your nunchaku (2-3).

AGAINST THE KNIFE

Face your opponent in a gedan suihei kamae stance (1). As your opponent thrusts at your body (2-3), raise your arms and step to the side (4-5). Strike at the side of his head (6).

Face your opponent in a gedan suihei kamae stance (1). As your opponent thrusts at your body, step to the side and bring your nunchaku to the side of the body. You will be in a jodan yoko kamae stance (2). Strike the outside of the knee (3-5).

Face your opponent in a gedan kamae stance (1). As your opponent thrusts at your body, raise the arms and step to the side (2). Strike the body upward and diagonally (3-4). Continue swinging the nunchaku above the opposite shoulder (5-6). Strike his neck diagonally and downward (7-8).

Face your opponent in a gedan suihei kamae stance (1). As your opponent goes for your head (2), raise your arms for a block (3). Push his arm down to the side (4). While he's off balance, thrust toward his throat with the butt of your weapon (5-7).

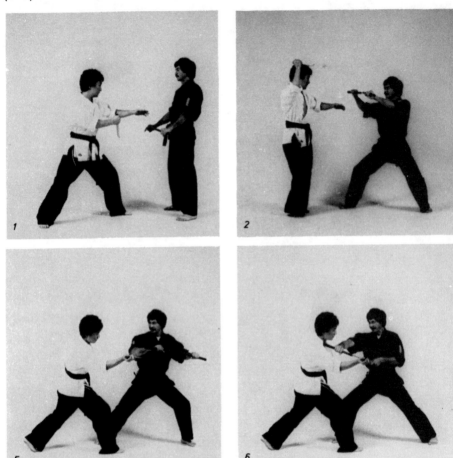

AGAINST EMPTY HAND

Face your opponent in a gedan suihei kamae stance (1). As your opponent moves, take a step backward (2). As your opponent punches your face (3), block to the outside with the forearm (4). Pull back the nunchaku (5) and strike the opponent's cheekbones with the butts of your nunchaku.

Face your opponent in a gedan katate yoko kamae stance (1). As your opponent kicks toward your lower body, step backward and raise your arm above your head (2). Twist your body and block to the outside with your nunchaku (3).

Face your opponent in a gedan katate stance (1). As your enemy attacks your midsection with a kick, step backward and hold the weapon in both hands (2). Push strongly down (3).

Face your opponent in a gedan suihei kamae stance (1). As your opponent moves to throw a kick, step backward and raise your arms (2). Block the shin with the butt ends of the nunchaku (3-5).

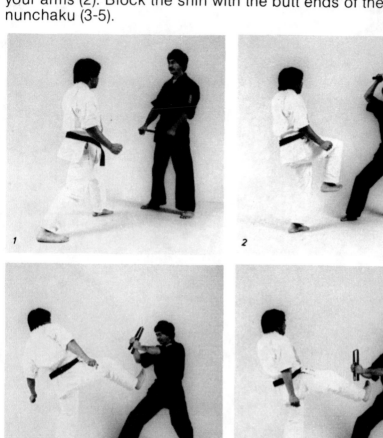

Face your opponent in a gedan suihei kamae stance (1). As your opponent attempts to strike you in the face, step backward, raise your arms (2) and strike his body at the ribcage area (3-4).

Face your opponent in a gedan suihei kamae stance (1). As your opponent tries to kick you in the midsection, step backward and raise the arms (2). Step to the side and strike the opponent's leg with the butt of the nunchaku (3).

Face your opponent in a gedan suihei kamae stance (1). As your opponent kicks at your body, step to the side, move your arms in a circular motion and hit his ankle bone with the butt of the weapon (2).

AGAINST THE BO

Face your opponent in a gedan suihei kamae stance (1). As your opponent goes for your head, step backward and block the strike above the head (2-3). Raise your arms higher and step forward, with the left foot pushing your opponent's staff to the ground (4-5). Twist your body and strike your enemy's face (6). Twist back and strike the opposite side of his face (7-8).

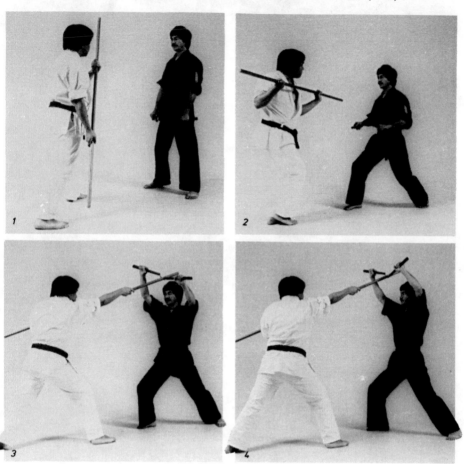

Continued

AGAINST THE BO

Face your opponent in a gedan suihei kamae stance (1). As your opponent strikes at the right side of your head, step to the left and block his bo (2-4). Duck under the bo and move through your opponent. At the same time, strike the enemy (5-7). Continue swinging the nunchaku in a circular upward motion (8-9). Strike down on the back of the opponent's neck (10-11).

Continued

Face your opponent in a gedan suihei kamae stance (1). As your opponent attacks your leg, step backward and raise your foot. Strike down on his bo to protect your leg (2-3). Raise your arm above the shoulder (4). Strike his neck (5-6). Retrieve the nunchaku with the opposite hand (7) and thrust into the side of his neck with your weapon (8-9).

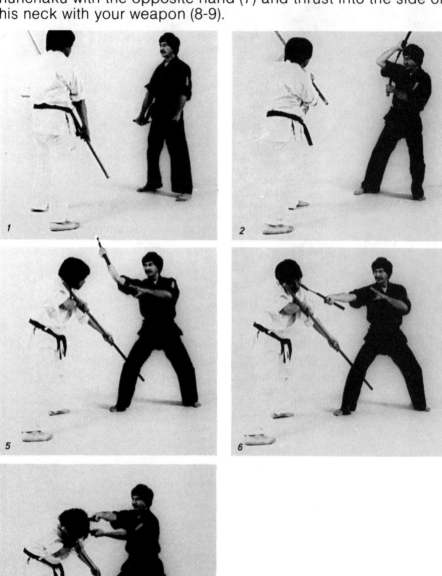

Face your opponent in a gedan suihei kamae stance (1). As your opponent strikes toward the left side of your neck (2), step forward to stop his bo (3). Strike his face three times with the edge of your nunchaku — right, then left, then right (4-6). Then strike his face with the butt of your weapon (7-8).

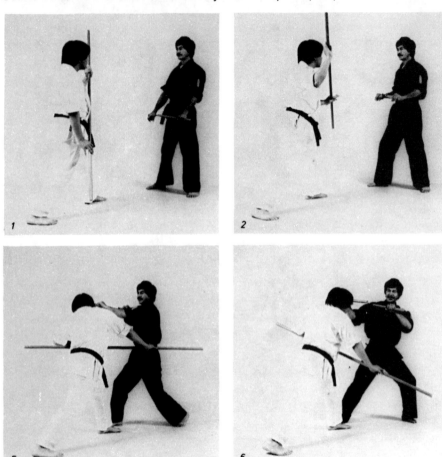

Face your opponent in a gedan suihei kamae stance (1). As your opponent thrusts at your throat (2), block his blow to the side (3). Twist your body and strike him with the left and right sides of your nunchaku (4-6).

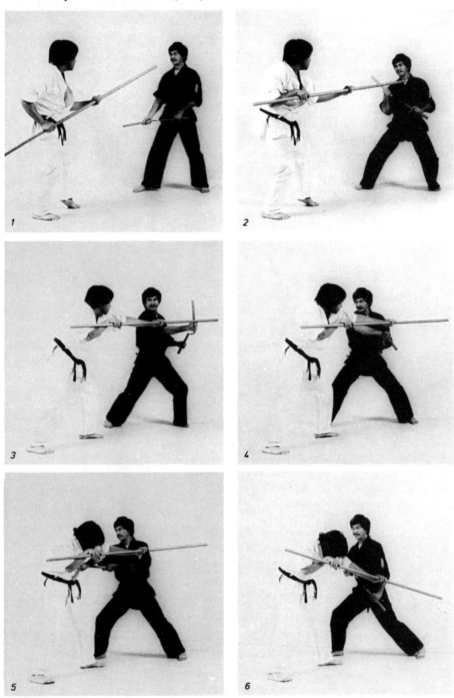

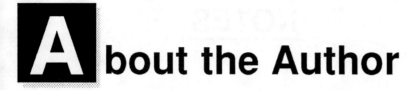

About the Author

Jiro Shiroma was born on the Ryukyu Islands (Okinawa) and began studying **shuri-te** (Okinawan old-style fighting arts) under master Kanji Inafuku.

At the age of 15, Shiroma took up **kendo** under Tokusei Yamashiro, who was an eighth-degree black belt. Shiroma received his first dan (black belt) three years later.

When he was 20, he started training in karate and kobudo under Shugiro Nakazato, tenth-dan leader and president of the Okinawan Shorin-Ryu Karate-Do Association.

In 1968, he received his sixth-degree black belt from grandmaster Chosun Chibana and was given the title "shihan," which meant certified instructor. Even with the new title, Shiroma felt there was much more to learn. In fact, he thought his knowledge was not sufficient enough to be called shihan.

One day he told master Nakazato about his dilemma and Nakazato took him aside. Master Nakazato then performed on Shiroma some movements and techniques he'd never shown to any student or class. These mysterious, unknown movements were his answer to Shiroma's dilemma. In essence, master Nakazato was saying martial arts is self-knowledge. Everyone's size, strength, and flexibility is different, so you have to develop your own movements and techniques based on what you've learned and experienced. You have to learn to apply a style's kata, as well as its variety of weapons. It is all up to the individual. This private lesson with one of the world's great martial artists taught Shiroma the true way of karate.

Shiroma began studying several martial arts to give him a more solid background. They included: **muay Thai** (Thai boxing), Western boxing, **tori-te** (similar to jiujitsu), and judo. The more experience he gained, the more comfortable he became with his title.

In 1976, he was granted a seventh-dan rank from master Nakazato and thus was called "kyoshi," or master instructor. A year later he moved to the United States and opened his first martial arts school in Phoenix, Ariz. He continues to teach there today.

NOTES

NOTES

NOTES

NOTES

NOTES

NOTES

NOTES

NOTES

NOTES